Hillstrom's Catalog Marketing PhD

A Doctorate Program in Multi-Channel Catalog Mailing Strategy for Highly
Advanced Catalog Marketers

Kevin Hillstrom

Acknowledgments

I would like to thank the catalog marketing community for having faith in the methodologies outlined in this booklet!

13 Digit ISBN: 978-1456463076

Published in the United States of America by Kevin Hillstrom

Available from Amazon.com and other retailers.

Manufactured in the United States of America
First Edition

Cover Design: Kevin Hillstrom and Createspace.com
Cover Art: Kevin Hillstrom and http://istockphoto.com

Biography

Kevin Hillstrom is a database marketing veteran with more than twenty years of experience analyzing customer behavior at many of America's greatest multichannel retailers.

Kevin began his professional career in 1998 as a Statistical Analyst at the Garst Seed Company, analyzing corn and sorghum trials.

In 1990, Kevin became a Statistical Analyst at Lands' End. It was at Lands' End where Kevin learned many of the tricks and techniques required to effectively model customer behavior. Kevin worked with a very bright direct marketing team, developing experiments that explained how customers interacted with different catalog titles over time, learning all about the ways that cannibalization of marketing activities erode company profitability. Kevin ended his tenure at Lands' End in late 1995, as Manager of Analytical Services.

In 1995, Kevin became Manager of Analytical Services at Eddie Bauer. Working with an integrated database (retail, catalog, online transactions), Kevin was able to demonstrate how customer behavior changed when new stores were opened in new markets, and how customer behavior changed when new stores were opened in existing markets. As Director of Circulation, Kevin partnered with a seasoned team of Executives to deliver the most profit ever generated by the direct-to-consumer division (catalog + internet), by reducing promotions (free shipping, % off offers), reducing catalog advertising to retail and online customers, and by using advanced statistical models to target customers with appropriate direct mail offerings. It was at Eddie Bauer that Kevin developed the methodologies that would ultimately become the foundation of "Multichannel Forensics".

Following a nine month stint as a Sr. Consultant at Avenue A, Kevin became Vice President of Direct Marketing at Nordstrom. The Executive team at Nordstrom Direct was charged with turning around a business that generated more than $300,000,000 in annual sales, but was losing more than $30,000,000 in profit each year. Within just two years, Kevin and his Executive team partners were able to re-calibrate catalog contact strategies and online marketing activities, bringing the business back to break-even.

In 2003, Kevin became Vice President of Database Marketing, working in the corporate office. Kevin's team was asked to integrate outbound customer marketing strategies (direct mail, catalogs, e-mail marketing), using an integrated transactional database. In 2004, Kevin was part of a team that decided to eliminate traditional catalog marketing, a decision that was widely criticized by purveyors of existing marketing best practices. In fact, Kevin was skeptical, too. However, within twelve months of eliminating a traditional catalog marketing program, retail comp store sales continued to increase, and without the support of catalog marketing, online sales actually increased at a rapid rate. It was at Nordstrom that the final touches were put on the "Multichannel Forensics" framework that accurately suggested that retail and online channels did not need catalog mailings to support sales growth.

In March 2007, Kevin left Nordstrom to begin his own consulting practice, called "MineThatData". Kevin utilizes his Multichannel Forensics framework to help marketers understand how customers interact with products, brands, and channels. Kevin's clients include online pure-plays, thirty million dollar catalog brands, billion dollar retail multichannel brands, and international direct marketers.

Following the collapse of the economy in 2007-2008, CEOs began asking different questions, questions that focused on the long-term sales trajectory of online advertising micro-channels. Kevin expanded his Multichannel Forensics framework, resulting in what are called "Online Marketing Simulations", tools that allows CEOs, CMOs, Online Marketers, and Web Analysts to understand how online and offline customers are likely to evolve and change in the future. This information allows the online marketer to identify the "Most Valuable Path", or "MVP", the path that maps how first time buyers become loyal customers. Armed with this information, investments in keyword campaigns, affiliate marketing, and e-mail marketing change, resulting in an improved and more profitable future.

And in 2010, CEOs asked a new set of questions, questions about customer behavior. Kevin created a new segmentation methodology called "Digital Profiles", designed to combine recency, frequency, and monetary information with the channels a customer purchases from, and the merchandise divisions a customer prefers, yielding sixteen actionable segments that can be used for targeting purposes, e-mail marketing strategy, catalog circulation strategy, online targeting, and general business intelligence.

Kevin also hosts the highly popular database marketing blog, called "The MineThatData Blog", where Kevin discusses online marketing, direct marketing, database marketing, and multichannel marketing topics on a frequent basis. You can also follow Kevin on Twitter!

Contact Information:

Kevin Hillstrom
E-Mail: kevinh@minethatdata.com
Website: http://minethatdata.com
Blog: http://blog.minethatdata.com
Twitter: http://twitter.com/minethatdata

Consulting Services

Kevin provides consulting services for leading online marketers and multichannel retailers. Given his experience at leading multichannel retailers like Nordstrom, Eddie Bauer, Lands' End, and more than four-dozen consultations with direct marketers and retailers, Kevin brings more than two decades of unique executive and analytical experience to his projects.

There are many popular projects that Kevin performs for CEOs and CMOs.

- Hashtag Analytics and Digital Profiles, social media segmentation projects resulting in actionable customer personas. The segments are used for a variety of customer targeting and business intelligence initiatives across social media, mobile initiatives, retailing, and e-commerce.

- Multichannel Forensics and Online Marketing Simulation Projects, designed to determine which customers no longer need to receive catalog mailings, and outline which customers should receive a mix of e-mail marketing and catalog marketing. A typical Multichannel Forensics Project for a $75,000,000 brand results in about $250,000 to $750,000 of annual profit opportunity, well worth the average cost of a Multichannel Forensics project. A typical Multichannel Forensics or Online Marketing Simulation project takes four weeks to complete, and costs between $10,000 and $40,000, depending upon how many twelve-month buyers your business manages.

- Price Elasticity Projects, where we determine how many units of an item will sell, given different pricing strategies. You will learn which price generates the most gross margin dollars for a given item, and you will receive a spreadsheet that allows you to play with different scenarios.

- Database Marketing Audits, designed to help the CEO/CMO understand how your business stacks up against competing organizations. The typical two-day audit results in a roadmap for success, outlining database strategies and marketing strategies and staffing strategies that yield profitable outcomes.

Contact me (kevinh@minethatdata.com) for project details.

Introduction

Matchbacks.

In theory, the concept of a "matchback" is good. We mailed a catalog to 1,000,000 households on November 1, 2002. Orders rolled-in via the telephone. We liked telephone orders, because they were easy to track and measure, telephone orders generally didn't happen unless a catalog was mailed to a customer.

Online orders trickled-in as well. A few days later, online orders surged.

The logical conclusion was that online orders happened because the catalog was mailed. Technology helped us understand this dynamic by matching the name and address of the person placing an online order to the file of customers mailed the catalog on November 1, 2002.

In the early days of the internet, customers generally didn't order online unless they were motivated by some form of advertising. The "matchback" proved that online orders happened because of catalog marketing.

Once our industry proved that catalogs caused online orders, we stopped our research. Instead of building upon our knowledge base by learning whether customer behavior changed and evolved over time, we instituted the "matchback" as a "best practice".

Oh boy.

In 2011, customers behave in ways we couldn't fathom in 2002. E-commerce, by and large, is a mature and stable medium. The customer knows you have an e-commerce website, heck, she's used the website for more than a decade, and is perfectly comfortable with the functionality of your website. Because she knows that your website exists, she doesn't necessarily have to be reminded that your website exists. In other words, your customer can choose to visit your website whenever she wishes.

Look at your own behavior. How often have you had an interest in purchasing a book, resulting in a visit to www.amazon.com? Amazon didn't have to advertise to you, they simply had to be there to capture your order.

This order that you place at Amazon is called an "organic" order ... no print advertising was required to cause the order to happen, the order happened for other reasons.

This situation happens today, in your catalog business. Customers visit your website, unprompted by advertising, visiting because of need, placing orders that are "organic" in nature.

Repeatedly, we "matchback" these organic orders to catalogs we sent to the customer. We give the catalog credit for an order that would have happened anyway.

This is a mistake, a big mistake.

The "matchback" causes us to over-state the performance of catalog marketing. When we over-state the performance of catalog marketing, we plan to mail too many catalogs next year, causing us to lose profit next year.

Profit is the lifeblood of business. Profit is the outcome of countless tactics and actions. Not surprisingly, when you increase profit, you increase your ability to invest in strategies, old-school strategies like catalog marketing, modern strategies like social media, and futuristic strategies like mobile.

By allocating organic orders, orders that would have happened without the aid of catalog marketing back to a catalog, we cause ourselves to spend money needlessly next year, we simply plan to mail catalogs to customers who will not use the catalogs to generate sales next year. In 2002, matchbacks caused you to generate significantly more profit, because you were able to match online orders that were caused by catalog marketing. In 2011, matchbacks cause you to generate less profit, because orders are incorrectly matched to catalog marketing activities.

My goal in life is to help you generate more profit. I am agnostic to channels (though I have an affinity for catalog marketers, given my employment history), I only care about making sure that your marketing efforts are as profitable as they can be.

In this small but important booklet, I will introduce you to an advanced methodology for determining the optimal number of catalogs to send to a customer. I've used this methodology with numerous catalog clients over the past two years, finding it to be an effective way to significantly increase profitability.

For almost no cost whatsoever, you're about to embark on a mission that may result in an increase in company profit of ten percent, or fifty percent, or even one-hundred percent! Come along with me as we explore a methodology that allows us to send an optimal number of catalogs to our customer base.

The Migration Probability Table

Let's begin our project by analyzing the Migration Probability Table for a sample company. This catalog company has four channels that it likes to analyze:

- Telephone: Orders taken over the phone (almost all generated by catalog mailings).
- E-Mail: Orders placed after a customer clicks-through an e-mail marketing campaign.
- Search: Paid and natural search orders placed after a customer clicks-through an ad on Google or Bing.
- Online: All other online orders.

Here's what the Migration Probability Table looks like for the catalog business we are about to analyze:

Migration Probability Table

		Overall	Phone	Online	E-Mail	Search
Rebuy Rates	Rebuy Rate	43.7%	46.1%	46.4%	55.9%	46.8%
	Phone		31.8%	7.6%	7.1%	7.1%
	Online		18.7%	34.3%	33.7%	29.6%
	E-Mail		8.2%	16.8%	35.9%	17.4%
	Search		4.4%	6.9%	8.0%	18.1%
Index	Phone		68.9%	16.4%	12.7%	15.1%
	Online		40.6%	73.9%	60.2%	63.2%
	E-Mail		17.9%	36.2%	64.1%	37.0%
	Search		9.6%	14.9%	14.2%	38.7%

Take a look at the "E-Mail" column. 55.9% of last year's e-mail customers purchased again this year, that's a good thing! The next four rows illustrate the percentage of last year's customers who purchased next year in each of the four channels.

Most important are the four rows next to the "Index" statement. Here, we take the rebuy rate for, say, "Search" among E-Mail customers (8.0%), and divide it by the overall Rebuy Rate (55.9%), yielding an index of 14.2%.

The index is categorized in three modes:
- Isolation Mode: An index of 0% to 19%.
- Equilibrium Mode: An index of 20% to 49%.
- Transfer Mode: An index of 50% or greater.

If a catalog brand has a telephone channel that is in Equilibrium/Transfer with the online channel, and the online channel is in Isolation with other channels, then we have a business that is likely to have many organic orders (orders not caused by catalog marketing) in the future.

This is a business that is likely to have a lot of organic orders in the future.

Search customers are most likely to order next from the online channel.

E-Mail customers are equally likely to purchase via e-mail or the online channel, and are not likely to buy via the telephone, or via search. This means that once a customer purchases via e-mail marketing, the customer has made a switch away from catalog marketing, yielding many opportunities to reduce catalog contacts.

Online customers tend to stay in the online channel, yielding a fertile ground for catalog frequency testing.

Telephone customers are most likely to stay within the telephone channel, though many are likely to migrate online. These customers are probably not very "organic", meaning that they need catalogs to be mailed to them in order to generate future demand and profit.

The Migration Probability Table is very useful, because it helps us understand how likely customers are to migrate between channels. In this case, we learn that customers have a natural gravity that pulls them to the online channel. Customers, ultimately, are being pulled away from traditional catalog marketing. We will have opportunities to change the number of contacts we mail to customers, opportunities that will yield healthy increases in company profitability. Had we observed that online customers migrated back to telephone orders, or had we observed that e-mail customers migrated back to telephone orders, we would not have had a reason to continue down the path of optimization, because customers were demonstrating to us that the catalog was the primary reason for purchasing.

Digital Profiles

The next step in the analysis is the creation of sixteen "Digital Profiles". Digital Profiles are simply segments of customers, based on customer behavior during the past twelve months.

The methodology is a bit more advanced than the analytics we're used to seeing. At a high level, I will describe the methodology.

In this analysis, I am focusing on a set of key variables, variables that represent customer behavior during a twelve-month period of time.

- Demand = Amount spent in the past twelve months.
- Frequency = Orders in the past twelve months.
- Items = Items purchased in the past twelve months.
- Price per Item = Price per item purchased.
- Items per Order = Items purchased per order.
- Telephone = 1/0 indicator telling if customer ordered via telephone in the past year.
- Online = 1/0 indicator telling if customer ordered via online channel in the past year.
- E-Mail = 1/0 indicator telling if customer ordered via e-mail marketing in the past year.
- Search = 1/0 indicator telling if customer ordered via search marketing in the past year.
- Product A = 1/0 indicator telling if customer purchased from product category "A" in the past year.
- Product B = 1/0 indicator telling if customer purchased from product category "B" in the past year.
- Product C = 1/0 indicator telling if customer purchased from product category "C" in the past year.
- Product D = 1/0 indicator telling if customer purchased from product category "D" in the past year.
- Low Price = 1/0 indicator telling if customer purchased an item in the past year in the "lowest third" of the company pricing tier.
- Average Price = 1/0 indicator telling if customer purchased an item in the past year in the "middle third" of the company pricing tier.
- High Price = 1/0 indicator telling if customer purchased an item in the past year in the "highest third" of the company pricing tier.
- Geography Catalog + = 1/0 indicator telling if customer lives in a geography that prefers catalog marketing and performs at an above-average level.
- Geography Catalog = 1/0 indicator telling if customer lives in a geography that prefers catalog marketing and performs at an average level.
- Geography Catalog - = 1/0 indicator telling if customer lives in a geography that prefers catalog marketing and performs at a below-average level.
- Geography Online + = 1/0 indicator telling if customer lives in a geography that prefers ordering online and performs at an above-average level.
- Geography Online = 1/0 indicator telling if customer lives in a geography that prefers ordering online and performs at an average level.

- Geography Online - = 1/0 indicator telling if customer lives in a geography that prefers ordering online and performs at a below-average level.

I create a database that captures these variables for each twelve-month period of time. For the past twelve months, this is what the descriptive statistics looked like for each variable, across all customers purchasing in the past twelve months:

Descriptive Statistics

	N	Mean	Std. Deviation
Demand	109966	184.4991	271.86104
Frequency	109966	1.80	1.413
Items	109966	5.74	6.912
Price per Item	109966	37.6735	26.46409
Items per Order	109966	3.0400	2.49444
Telephone	109966	.240020	.4270970
Online	109966	.600658	.4897653
E-Mail	109966	.261244	.4393148
Search	109966	.144772	.3518724
Product A	109966	.417456	.4931417
Product B	109966	.659258	.4739608
Product C	109966	.284170	.4510201
Product D	109966	.003919	.0624825
Low Price	109966	.490470	.4999114
Avg Price	109966	.745394	.4356415
High Price	109966	.428305	.4948354
Geography Catalog +	109966	.059373	.2363224
Geography Catalog	109966	.101195	.3015880
Geography Catalog -	109966	.258471	.4377961
Geography Online +	109966	.139989	.3469769
Geography Online	109966	.211665	.4084907
Geography Online -	109966	.229307	.4203891
Valid N (listwise)	109966		

I have 109,966 customers who purchased in the past twelve months, and I now have the mean and standard deviation for each variable in the database. The mean and standard deviation will become important later in the creation of Digital Profiles.

Next, I will use a subset of variables in a Factor Analysis. My goal is to create four factors that describe the general behavior of customers. Let's look at the Rotated Component Matrix that is output from the Factor Analysis. I'll describe what the numbers mean next.

Rotated Component Matrix[a]

| | Component | | | |
	1	2	3	4
Frequency	.789	.347	.065	-.028
Telephone	-.006	.054	.086	.714
Online	.072	.142	.045	-.746
E-Mail	.538	.035	-.056	-.004
Search	.112	.036	-.059	.131
Product A	.273	-.102	-.840	-.024
Product B	.347	-.146	.848	.048
Product C	.063	.794	-.078	.034
Product D	.050	.145	-.071	-.015
Low Price	.562	.059	.069	-.027
Avg Price	.522	-.366	-.061	.015
High Price	.025	.772	.227	.040
Geography Catalog +	-.022	.028	-.002	.070
Geography Catalog	.003	-.011	.019	.081
Geography Catalog -	.029	.017	-.035	.428
Geography Online +	-.012	.036	-.044	-.172
Geography Online	-.013	-.048	.065	-.365

Extraction Method: Principal Component Analysis.
Rotation Method: Varimax with Kaiser Normalization.
  a. Rotation converged in 5 iterations.

In the table, any number that has an absolute value greater than 0.2 is an important component of a given factor.

In the first factor, the following variables are important.
- Frequency
- E-Mail
- Product A
- Product B
- Low Price
- Average Price
- These are customers who order often, who order via e-mail marketing, who buy products "A" and "B", and tend to buy inexpensive merchandise.

Here are the variables that are important in the second factor.
- Frequency
- Product C
- Average Price (Negative)
- High Price
- These are customers who order often, who purchase from product "C", and tend to buy high-priced items.

Here are the variables that are important in the third factor.
- Product A (Negative)
- Product B
- High Price
- These are customers who buy product "B" and not product "A", and tend to buy high-priced items.

Here are the variables that are important in the fourth factor.
- Telephone
- Online (Negative)
- Geography = Catalog –
- Geography = Online (Negative)
- In other words, these are pure catalog customers, customers not likely to generate orders organically, customers who require catalog marketing to purchase merchandise.

Now, what I am about to do would be blasted by statistical purists (if they didn't already criticize my use of a Factor Analysis) as being inappropriate. Too bad! I am not trying to find a cure for cancer, instead, I am trying to identify segments of customers who may or may not be responsive to catalog advertising!

Here's what comes next:
- I standardize each variable in my dataset, using the means and standard deviations outlined in an earlier table.

- I then use the Component Score Coefficient Matrix from the Factor Analysis Output to score each customer for each factor. Here's the Component Score Coefficient Matrix for our dataset.

Component Score Coefficient Matrix

	Component			
	1	2	3	4
Frequency	.442	.180	.004	-.005
Telephone	.004	.034	.036	.492
Online	.019	.083	.041	-.515
E-Mail	.316	-.003	-.055	.009
Search	.068	.021	-.048	.095
Product A	.190	-.042	-.559	.010
Product B	.187	-.151	.557	.017
Product C	-.002	.513	-.091	.030
Product D	.024	.094	-.054	-.007
Low Price	.324	.005	.027	-.010
Avg Price	.328	-.261	-.039	.020
High Price	-.031	.487	.113	.025
Geography Catalog +	-.013	.020	-.004	.049
Geography Catalog	.003	-.008	.011	.055
Geography Catalog -	.025	.013	-.036	.298
Geography Online +	-.011	.025	-.026	-.118
Geography Online	-.014	-.035	.055	-.254

Extraction Method: Principal Component Analysis.
Rotation Method: Varimax with Kaiser Normalization.
Component Scores.

Each coefficient above is multiplied by each standardized value for each customer, yielding the score for each of the four factors.

Next, I run a frequency distribution for each factor, identifying the median value for each factor:

Statistics

		REGR factor score 1 for analysis 1	REGR factor score 2 for analysis 1	REGR factor score 3 for analysis 1	REGR factor score 4 for analysis 1
N	Valid	109966	109966	109966	109966
	Missing	0	0	0	0
Percentiles	50	-.1017390	-.1651026	.0820727	-.1021764

Having identified each median, I categorize each customer as being above average (1) or below average (0) for each factor.

By doing this, I have 2*2*2*2 = 16 segment combinations for each customer. Each customer is assigned to one of sixteen segments, segments that I call "Digital Profiles".

Digital Profiles are important, because they are used to predict who is likely to generate organic orders, and they are used to predict who is likely to generate orders caused by catalog advertising.

I realize that this might be a complicated process ... that's why this is a PhD level course in catalog marketing, and that's why many clients hire me to help them work through this process. We've been conditioned to settle for easy, fast, and convenient solutions.

The outcome of the analysis, however, is worth it!

Sixteen Digital Profiles

Let's review the first four Digital Profiles.

Digital Profile -->	1	2	3	4
Households	7,970	6,883	7,971	6,958
Annual Demand	$370.38	$390.78	$432.24	$444.50
Annual Items	10.811	11.538	13.545	13.981
Annual Orders	3.089	3.281	3.462	3.667
Price per Item	$35.71	$35.84	$33.33	$33.59
Items per Order	3.865	3.841	4.214	4.057
Phone	49.5%	6.7%	50.0%	4.5%
Online	45.6%	95.9%	49.0%	95.3%
E-Mail	41.8%	43.1%	44.3%	51.0%
Search	19.5%	13.6%	21.6%	18.5%
Product A	2.0%	5.8%	98.0%	98.0%
Product B	100.0%	100.0%	68.9%	69.7%
Product C	56.6%	50.4%	68.1%	65.9%
Product D	0.2%	0.3%	1.5%	2.5%
Low Price	81.0%	82.1%	78.9%	81.5%
Avg Price	94.4%	95.4%	95.6%	95.5%
High Price	81.8%	86.2%	77.7%	77.8%
Geo = Catalog +	5.6%	5.8%	5.8%	6.8%
Geo = Catalog	9.2%	10.4%	8.9%	11.7%
Geo = Catalog -	47.9%	0.5%	49.7%	0.7%
Geo = Online +	11.1%	16.6%	11.8%	19.5%
Geo = Online	7.3%	39.7%	5.9%	32.5%
Geo = Online -	18.8%	26.9%	17.9%	28.8%

The data suggests that the fourth Digital Profile was the most valuable last year, spending $444.50, buying a total of 3.667 times.

Notice that the second and fourth Digital Profiles are online-centric, whereas the first and third Digital Profiles have a propensity for buying over the telephone. This is important, because we want to mail catalogs to only the customers most likely to respond to catalogs. In most of my projects, customers shopping via the telephone channel are most likely to respond to catalog mailings!

Take a look at the merchandise that customers purchase. The biggest difference is in Product "A". The first two Digital Profiles do not buy this merchandise, whereas the third and fourth Digital Profiles do buy this merchandise.

Also notice that the first and third Digital Profiles, with customers who are likely to purchase via the telephone, are comprised of customers who live in geographical areas that possess customers who love catalog marketing but spend below-average amounts of money. Here, I'm using my Zip Code Forensics data to infer my findings. You are free to use whatever data you have available about geographical customer behavior.

Here's the data for Digital Profiles five, six, seven, and eight.

Digital Profile -->	5	6	7	8
Households	6,545	6,441	6,680	6,162
Annual Demand	$112.81	$134.01	$139.93	$162.08
Annual Items	4.702	5.922	5.811	7.026
Annual Orders	1.467	1.792	1.675	2.017
Price per Item	$25.25	$23.39	$25.27	$23.85
Items per Order	3.378	3.557	3.686	3.723
Phone	28.7%	1.5%	29.9%	2.1%
Online	10.7%	78.1%	18.3%	81.6%
E-Mail	63.1%	43.6%	59.9%	42.6%
Search	15.5%	6.0%	18.4%	9.4%
Product A	0.7%	0.5%	100.0%	100.0%
Product B	100.0%	100.0%	46.0%	43.1%
Product C	0.0%	0.2%	0.2%	0.2%
Product D	0.0%	0.0%	0.0%	0.0%
Low Price	69.3%	85.5%	64.5%	79.0%
Avg Price	84.6%	89.6%	88.5%	92.9%
High Price	7.6%	3.4%	4.1%	0.8%
Geo = Catalog +	6.6%	4.4%	6.3%	4.3%
Geo = Catalog	13.3%	8.1%	11.7%	8.4%
Geo = Catalog -	34.9%	16.9%	37.7%	10.9%
Geo = Online +	10.8%	13.4%	12.8%	15.1%
Geo = Online	7.6%	37.3%	6.2%	39.1%
Geo = Online -	26.7%	19.9%	25.3%	22.3%

Recall that Digital Profiles one, two, three, and four spent more than three hundred dollars each. These four Digital Profiles only spent $113 to $162 last year.

Notice that customers in these Digital Profiles buy inexpensive items. Notice that customers in these Digital Profiles have a preference for e-mail marketing. This is a common finding ... cheap items and/or discounts/promotions and e-mail marketing are frequently correlated. We spent the past decade trying so hard to get customers to respond to e-mail marketing, ending up in a race to the bottom, where low price and deals rule e-mail marketing. In so many of my projects, the e-mail customer is a good customer, a really good customer, but is a customer reliant on deals.

Again, two Digital Profiles prefer Product "B" and two Digital Profiles prefer Product "A". We've yet to run across a Digital Profile that has an affinity for Product "C".

Next, we will study Digital Profiles nine, ten, eleven, and twelve. The tone shifts as we evaluate the remaining eight Digital Profiles.

Here, then, are Digital Profiles nine through twelve.

Digital Profile -->	9	10	11	12
Households	6,407	5,300	6,971	7,111
Annual Demand	$149.87	$156.74	$123.58	$125.22
Annual Items	2.865	3.089	2.237	2.348
Annual Orders	1.249	1.256	1.121	1.138
Price per Item	$59.65	$58.17	$70.23	$66.98
Items per Order	2.332	2.488	1.994	2.041
Phone	53.0%	1.9%	41.8%	0.8%
Online	28.7%	97.6%	26.8%	95.2%
E-Mail	7.9%	3.4%	15.3%	5.7%
Search	19.5%	4.8%	22.4%	2.6%
Product A	0.2%	0.5%	30.7%	36.1%
Product B	100.0%	100.0%	4.5%	3.2%
Product C	25.8%	22.2%	81.1%	73.0%
Product D	0.0%	0.2%	0.5%	1.1%
Low Price	12.7%	14.2%	15.4%	23.1%
Avg Price	41.4%	46.7%	30.5%	25.2%
High Price	96.0%	96.0%	79.0%	72.5%
Geo = Catalog +	6.3%	7.0%	6.2%	8.3%
Geo = Catalog	7.7%	11.9%	8.9%	10.0%
Geo = Catalog -	47.0%	2.0%	44.8%	5.4%
Geo = Online +	11.4%	18.3%	12.2%	20.8%
Geo = Online	10.6%	32.0%	10.8%	28.7%
Geo = Online -	17.2%	28.8%	17.1%	26.8%

The first thing you notice are the price points … these are customers who purchase expensive items!! And for the first time, you see Product "C". If you are a marketer targeting Product "C", you focus on Digital Profiles eleven and twelve.

Again, telephone customers are heavily skewed to the "odd numbered" Digital Profiles. Notice that e-mail doesn't make up a large percentage of the customer base in these four Digital Profiles … there is a clear correlation between low price points and e-mail marketing preference.

Finally, we evaluate the last four Digital Profiles, thirteen through sixteen.

Digital Profile -->	13	14	15	16
Households	7,649	8,076	4,952	8,496
Annual Demand	$69.49	$59.05	$81.61	$70.11
Annual Items	2.332	2.457	2.789	2.560
Annual Orders	1.073	1.108	1.063	1.061
Price per Item	$31.09	$26.39	$30.09	$28.71
Items per Order	2.181	2.221	2.641	2.422
Phone	55.3%	0.7%	61.8%	0.4%
Online	21.6%	98.4%	4.7%	98.9%
E-Mail	0.0%	0.0%	0.0%	0.0%
Search	26.0%	2.8%	36.3%	1.8%
Product A	0.0%	0.0%	100.0%	100.0%
Product B	100.0%	100.0%	12.1%	6.9%
Product C	0.0%	0.0%	0.0%	0.0%
Product D	0.0%	0.0%	0.0%	0.0%
Low Price	19.7%	36.5%	15.6%	20.4%
Avg Price	80.3%	63.5%	84.4%	79.6%
High Price	5.5%	0.0%	3.2%	1.1%
Geo = Catalog +	4.9%	6.7%	7.2%	4.0%
Geo = Catalog	10.6%	10.6%	11.6%	9.8%
Geo = Catalog -	41.0%	11.1%	29.5%	24.0%
Geo = Online +	9.8%	16.3%	13.4%	12.0%
Geo = Online	15.7%	27.6%	17.5%	25.3%
Geo = Online -	18.0%	27.7%	20.9%	25.0%

Here, we find four Digital Profiles that are comprised of customers who only purchased about one time last year, and when they purchased, they purchased inexpensive items from Product "A" and Product "B".

Later, we'll learn that these customers are not likely to purchase again in the next twelve months. That's an important finding, because if these customers are being mailed a lot of catalogs, we'll want to cut back here and save money.

There are several things I want for you to take away from our review of sixteen Digital Profiles.
- Product "A" buyers are skewed to Digital Profiles 3/4/7/8/15/16.
- Product "B" buyers are skewed to Digital Profiles 1/2/5/6/9/10/13/14, with some coverage in Digital Profiles 3/4/7/8.

- Product "C" buyers are skewed to Digital Profiles 11/12, with some coverage in Digital Profiles 1/2/3/4/9/10.
- Telephone shoppers are in Digital Profiles 1/3/5/7/9/11/13/15 (catalog focused).
- Online shoppers are in Digital Profiles 2/4/6/8/10/12/14/16 (likely to be more organic in nature, requiring fewer catalogs).
- E-Mail shoppers are in Digital Profiles 1/2/3/4/5/6/7/8.
- Search shoppers are NOT in Digital Profiles 6/8/10/12/14/16.
- High Price Point shoppers are in Digital Profiles 9/10/11/12.

At this point, you might be asking yourself "What do Digital Profiles have to do with determining how many catalogs to send to a customer?"

Well, it turns out that one can take dozens or hundreds of variables, reduce the dimensionality (as we did here), and then use the information in a modeling process designed to determine how many catalogs to mail to a customer!

The Modeling Process

There are three models that I create, when identifying how many catalogs to send to a customer on an annual basis.

In this example, I am going to use twenty-four months of purchase history to predict what a customer is likely to do in the next twelve months. I've worked on projects where I use fifteen or more years of purchase data, I've worked on projects where I only use twelve months of purchase history. Use the data you have available to you, apply the concepts outlined here to your situation.

The first model that I create is a probability model. I use Logistic Regression to predict the likelihood of a customer purchasing in the next twelve months, regardless of channel.

In this example, I use many unique variables.
- Square Root of Months Since Last Purchase.
- Number of Purchases 0-12 Months Ago.
- Number of Purchases 13-24 Months Ago.
- 1/0 Indicators for Each of Sixteen Digital Profiles a Customer Belonged to in Past Year.
- 1/0 Indicators for Each of Sixteen Digital Profiles a Customer Belonged to 13-24 Months Ago.

You're free to use whatever variables you want to use. I know of statistical experts that like to use hundreds of variables, and I've observed significant success in those situations. I know of statistical experts that like to use three or four variables, and I've observed success in those situations.

I came to the conclusion that a hybrid of each approach makes the most sense. I try to reduce the dimensionality of a ton of correlated variables by using a combination of Factor Analysis and Segmentation (called Digital Profiles), and then I try to use as few variables as possible (recency + frequency + Digital Profiles).

You, of course, are free to do whatever is right for your customer!

Here is the outcome of the model I created to predict the likelihood of a customer purchasing in the next twelve months:

Variables in the Equation

		B	S.E.	Wald	df	Sig.	Exp(B)
Step 1[a]	root_rec	-.361	.010	1431.859	1	.000	.697
	hst_frq12	.324	.008	1535.820	1	.000	1.383
	hst_frq99	.141	.007	450.446	1	.000	1.151
	hst_dp12			563.365	16	.000	
	hst_dp12(1)	.446	.038	140.798	1	.000	1.561
	hst_dp12(2)	.444	.041	119.460	1	.000	1.558
	hst_dp12(3)	.414	.038	115.688	1	.000	1.512
	hst_dp12(4)	.512	.042	147.898	1	.000	1.669
	hst_dp12(5)	.297	.035	73.269	1	.000	1.346
	hst_dp12(6)	.478	.037	170.816	1	.000	1.612
	hst_dp12(7)	.408	.035	133.844	1	.000	1.504
	hst_dp12(8)	.441	.038	133.383	1	.000	1.555
	hst_dp12(9)	.252	.034	55.180	1	.000	1.287
	hst_dp12(10)	.250	.037	45.882	1	.000	1.284
	hst_dp12(11)	-.032	.034	.907	1	.341	.968
	hst_dp12(12)	-.092	.036	6.652	1	.010	.912
	hst_dp12(13)	.140	.033	18.259	1	.000	1.150
	hst_dp12(14)	.189	.033	32.116	1	.000	1.208
	hst_dp12(15)	.092	.038	5.948	1	.015	1.096
	hst_dp12(16)	.122	.034	13.116	1	.000	1.130
	hst_dp99			1219.136	16	.000	
	hst_dp99(1)	.811	.034	563.163	1	.000	2.249
	hst_dp99(2)	.799	.037	459.017	1	.000	2.223
	hst_dp99(3)	.767	.035	490.016	1	.000	2.154
	hst_dp99(4)	.784	.038	425.709	1	.000	2.189
	hst_dp99(5)	.674	.030	492.658	1	.000	1.963
	hst_dp99(6)	.657	.032	414.726	1	.000	1.928
	hst_dp99(7)	.719	.032	513.417	1	.000	2.053
	hst_dp99(8)	.739	.035	458.619	1	.000	2.094
	hst_dp99(9)	.616	.033	358.079	1	.000	1.851
	hst_dp99(10)	.504	.037	185.406	1	.000	1.656
	hst_dp99(11)	.356	.034	108.723	1	.000	1.427
	hst_dp99(12)	.320	.035	82.316	1	.000	1.377
	hst_dp99(13)	.460	.029	251.203	1	.000	1.585
	hst_dp99(14)	.404	.031	171.845	1	.000	1.498
	hst_dp99(15)	.448	.037	148.080	1	.000	1.565
	hst_dp99(16)	.307	.034	82.993	1	.000	1.360
	Constant	-.681	.043	246.836	1	.000	.506

a. Variable(s) entered on step 1: root_rec, hst_frq12, hst_frq99, hst_dp12, hst_dp99.

Root_rec is the square root of recency. Hst_frq12 is the number of orders in the past 12 months, while hst_frq99 is the number of orders 13-24 months ago.

Hst_dp12 represents the Digital Profile that a customer belonged to in the last twelve months, while hst_dp99 represents the Digital Profile that a customer belonged to 13-24 months ago … each row in the table shows the coefficient (labeled "B") for customers who possess that segment assignment.

Let's take an example. Say a customer has a recency of six months, purchased one time last year, purchased one time 13-24 months ago, belonged to Digital Profile #4 last year, and belonged to Digital Profile #12 13-24 months ago.
- Prediction = -0.681 + 0.324*(hst_freq12) + 0.141*(hst_freq99) + 0.512*(0-12 Month Digital Profile #4) + 0.320*(13-24 Month Digital Profile #12).
- Prediction = -0.681 + 0.324*(1) + 0.141*(1) + 0.512*(1) + 0.320*(1).
- Prediction = 0.616.
- Prediction = EXP(0.616) / (1 + EXP(0.616).
- Prediction = 0.649.

A customer with this "resume" has a 64.9% chance of buying again in the next twelve months.

Next, I predict the amount of demand a customer will spend in the next twelve months. In this case, I use the following variables:
- Amount spent 0-12 months ago.
- Amount spent 13-24 months ago.
- 1/0 Indicators for Each of Sixteen Digital Profiles a Customer Belonged to in Past Year.
- 1/0 Indicators for Each of Sixteen Digital Profiles a Customer Belonged to 13-24 Months Ago.

I used a Stepwise Regression process. You are free to use whatever methodology you wish to use, and you are free to use any variable you think is appropriate.

Here's the outcome of my modeling process, using only customers who purchased in the next twelve months to predict spend in the next twelve months.

Coefficients[a]

Model		Unstandardized Coefficients		Standardized Coefficients		
		B	Std. Error	Beta	t	Sig.
1	(Constant)	129.033	1.299		99.361	.000
	hst_dmd12	.572	.004	.539	157.182	.000
2	(Constant)	109.314	1.313		83.267	.000
	hst_dmd12	.459	.004	.432	112.552	.000
	hst_dmd99	.226	.004	.217	56.499	.000
3	(Constant)	110.067	1.316		83.628	.000
	hst_dmd12	.466	.004	.440	110.983	.000
	hst_dmd99	.226	.004	.217	56.406	.000
	dp1204	-31.818	4.293	-.026	-7.411	.000
4	(Constant)	111.253	1.323		84.117	.000
	hst_dmd12	.478	.004	.450	108.531	.000
	hst_dmd99	.225	.004	.216	56.212	.000
	dp1204	-38.323	4.357	-.031	-8.796	.000
	dp1203	-34.879	4.063	-.030	-8.584	.000
5	(Constant)	112.704	1.355		83.200	.000
	hst_dmd12	.478	.004	.451	108.624	.000
	hst_dmd99	.224	.004	.215	56.124	.000
	dp1204	-39.856	4.367	-.032	-9.126	.000
	dp1203	-36.412	4.074	-.032	-8.937	.000
	dp1207	-23.115	4.683	-.017	-4.936	.000
6	(Constant)	114.065	1.385		82.362	.000
	hst_dmd12	.479	.004	.451	108.740	.000
	hst_dmd99	.224	.004	.215	56.038	.000
	dp1204	-41.446	4.379	-.034	-9.464	.000
	dp1203	-38.000	4.087	-.033	-9.297	.000
	dp1207	-24.535	4.691	-.018	-5.230	.000
	dp1208	-23.093	4.908	-.016	-4.705	.000
7	(Constant)	115.274	1.410		81.755	.000
	hst_dmd12	.485	.005	.457	105.435	.000
	hst_dmd99	.224	.004	.215	55.981	.000
	dp1204	-45.562	4.471	-.037	-10.190	.000
	dp1203	-42.079	4.184	-.037	-10.057	.000
	dp1207	-26.680	4.714	-.019	-5.659	.000
	dp1208	-25.353	4.933	-.017	-5.140	.000
	dp1201	-18.489	4.066	-.016	-4.547	.000

a. Dependent Variable: spend

28

Step 7 is the resulting model:

- Spend = \$115.274 + 0.485*(demand spent 0-12 months ago) + 0.224*(demand spent 13-24 months ago) – 45.562*(Digital Profile #4 0-12 Months Ago) – 42.079*(Digital Profile #3 0-12 Months Ago) – 26.680*(Digital Profile #7 0-12 Months Ago) – 25.353*(Digital Profile #8 0-12 Months Ago) – 18.489*(Digital Profile #1 0-12 Months Ago).

Let's take an example. Our customer purchased once last year, spending \$100, and purchased once 13-24 months ago, spending \$100. The customer belonged to Digital Profile #4 last year, and Digital Profile #12 13-24 months ago.

- Prediction = \$115.274 +0.485*(\$100) + 0.224*(\$100) – 45.562*(1).
- Prediction = \$140.612.

We now have two pieces of the puzzle.

- Probability of Buying Again, Next 12 Months = 64.9%.
- Predicted Spend, Next 12 Months = \$140.612.

The next step is to multiply these values together. By multiplying the values together, we know how much each customer will spend in the next year.

- Predicted Value = 0.649*140.612 = \$91.26.

This customer is predicted to spend \$91.26 next year.

We're down to the last step in the process. Here, I am going to predict how much of the \$91.26 in our example will be "organic", in other words, how much of the \$91.26 will be caused by anything other than catalog marketing!

The Organic Percentage

This, to me, is the most interesting part of the analysis.

In a perfect world, the catalog brand had the foresight to execute a long-term catalog mail/holdout test. In this example, a six month test was conducted. At the end of the six month process, I measured the results of the test.

- 100% of telephone demand is caused by catalog mailings.
- 50% of online demand is caused by catalog mailings.
- 10% of e-mail demand is caused by catalog mailings.
- 40% of search demand is caused by catalog mailings.

I have many clients who don't execute catalog mail/holdout tests, so I have to use proprietary methods to estimate the percentages. In this case, I have the actual percentages, so I will use them!

The "Organic Percentage" is the percentage of demand generated by all channels outside of the catalog channel. It is the converse of the metrics listed above.

So, in our example, we had a customer who purchased one time 0-12 months ago, and one time 13-24 months ago. The purchase 0-12 months ago was in the e-mail channel, the purchase 13-24 months ago was in the online channel. Each purchase was for $100.

Here are our rules, derived from mail/holdout testing.
- 0% of telephone demand is organic.
- 50% of online demand is organic.
- 90% of e-mail demand is organic.
- 60% of search demand is organic.

Historically, then, we have the following organic percentage:
- Organic Demand = $0.90*100 + 0.50*100 = \$140$.
- Total Demand = $\$100 + \$100 = \$200$.
- Organic Percentage = $\$140 / \$200 = 70\%$.

When I am predicting the Organic Percentage, I use historical organic percentage as an independent variable, and I use the Digital Profile a customer belonged to as a series of independent variables. The Digital Profiles are important, of course, because they are made up of combinations of channel preferences. If a Digital Profile is skewed to e-mail marketing, then that Digital Profile is likely to yield more "organic demand" in the next year than is a Digital Profile that is skewed to telephone orders.

I use a Logistic Regression model. Again, statistical purists are going to lambast me here, and I don't really care, I'm not trying to measure the effectiveness of a drug for a cancer trial.

Here's what I do. I start with a dependent variable ... Future Organic Percentage. This number is a percentage for each respondent ... 0% for some, 50% for some, 70% for some, 100% for some. Next, I use a random number generator, and if the random number is less than the future organic percentage, I code my dependent variable as "1", otherwise, it is "0". At this point, I can use Logistic Regression, having a dependent variable with a 1/0 definition.

Yes, I realize statistical purists will offer numerous transformations on a continuous variable that will work. Have at it, create something better than this! This is the methodology I am using. The methodology flat-out works.

Here's the equation:

- Predicted Organic Percentage = -1.304 + 2.979*(Historical Organic Percentage) – 0.033*(Square Root of Recency) – 0.157*(12 Month Digital Profile = 05) – 0.210*(12 Month Digital Profile = 09) + 0.162*(12 Month Digital Profile = 12) – 0.199*(12 Month Digital Profile = 13) + 0.174*(12 Month Digital Profile = 14) – 0.108*(13-24 Month Digital Profile = 03) – 0.186*(13-24 Month Digital Profile = 07).

Let's use our example … the customer had a 70% historical organic percentage, was in Digital Profile #4 last year, and was in Digital Profile #12 the year prior.

- Prediction = -1.304 + 2.979*(0.70).
- Prediction = .781.
- Transform: Prediction = EXP(0.781) / (1 + EXP(0.781)) = 68.6%

What Do We Know?

Well, we know four important pieces of information.

- Probability of Buying Again, Next 12 Months = 64.9%.
- Predicted Spend, Next 12 Months = $140.612.
- Predicted Value = 0.649*140.612 = $91.26.
- Predicted Organic Percentage = 68.6%.

If I know the predicted value for spend in the next year ($91.26), and I know the predicted organic percentage (68.6%), I know the amount that will be generated due to catalog marketing.

- Predicted Catalog Marketing Value = Predicted Value * (1 – Predicted Organic Percentage).
- Predicted Catalog Marketing Value = $91.26 * (1 – 68.6%).
- Predicted Catalog Marketing Value = $28.66.

This is the most important metric in all of catalog marketing (outside of the organic percentage).

What this means is that our sample customer will spend $91.26 in the next year, $28.66 due to catalog marketing, $62.60 due to all other factors.

Most catalog marketers mistakenly attribute all $91.26 to catalog marketing efforts via the "matchback" process. This causes catalog marketers to, at times, significantly over-circulate catalogs to customers.

What do we know? We know how much the customer is likely to spend next year, due to catalog marketing. Now, we need to know how many catalogs we should send to customers. We can figure this out!

The Ranking Table

After I finish creating the models, I score every customer as of one year ago. Then I rank-order the customer base, in order from highest catalog marketing value score to lowest catalog marketing value score.

For reporting purposes, I like to use small segments of customers, 1% or 2% of the customer file in each segment. I average predicted catalog marketing value scores, I average actual catalog marketing demand, I average organic demand, I average profit, I average the number of catalogs mailed, and I average profit per customer in the small segment.

For the purposes of this booklet, I will use ranking deciles. Here's what the table looks like for last year:

Decile	HHs	Prediction	Fut. Catlg.	Fut. Orgn.	Fut. Demd.	Mailed	Profit
1	17,671	$191.16	$193.38	$152.64	$346.02	14.3	$111.09
2	17,670	$67.99	$67.73	$68.26	$135.99	13.7	$37.99
3	17,671	$41.90	$44.60	$47.16	$91.76	13.1	$22.94
4	17,670	$29.61	$31.43	$31.85	$63.28	12.3	$13.54
5	17,671	$22.71	$23.31	$24.27	$47.58	11.5	$8.62
6	17,670	$18.26	$19.44	$20.39	$39.83	10.6	$6.54
7	17,671	$14.94	$15.27	$17.57	$32.84	9.8	$4.65
8	17,670	$12.17	$12.26	$16.31	$28.57	10.0	$2.99
9	17,671	$9.61	$9.87	$12.70	$22.57	7.9	$2.38
10	17,670	$6.98	$8.52	$13.32	$21.83	7.0	$2.76
			Total Catalog Demand		$6,753,938		
			Total Organic Demand		$7,147,239		
			Total Demand		$13,901,177		
			Total Catalogs Mailed		1,946,230		
			Total Catalog Cost		$1,362,361		
			Total Profit		$3,772,695		

So things look pretty good, right?

Right?

Well, maybe things don't look quite as good as they appear.

Many catalog companies execute frequency tests. They analyze the relative gain in demand and profit achieved as a customer migrates from zero to one to two, on up to fifteen catalogs (or however many catalogs your brand mails in the course of a year). In my projects, we identify a relationship of diminishing returns … as catalog frequency increases, catalog demand increases, but at an ever-decreasing rate.

Let's explore this dynamic. In our example, the catalog brand mails fifteen catalogs a year. Look at the fifth decile. Here, customers receive an average of 11.5 catalog mailings a year.

What would happen if we mailed different combinations of mailings to this audience? Using a relationship of diminishing returns, I can simulate the outcome.

For some of my clients, the diminishing returns relationship can be approximated by the "square root rule". Here's what we do:
- Identify number of catalogs you want to simulate (say 5).
- Identify number of catalogs the customer was mailed last year (say 11.5).
- Calculate the square root of simulated catalogs vs. catalogs mailed last year:
  - $((5.0) / (11.5))$ ^ $0.5 = 0.659$.
  - Sending 5 catalogs yields 65.9% of the demand you'd get when mailing 11.5 catalogs.
- Multiply catalog demand by the percentage obtained in the square root simulation, then add organic demand, yielding total demand.
  - $\$23.31 * 0.659 + \$24.47 = \$39.64$.
- Calculate profit (here's a simplified formula in our example):
  - $\$39.64 * 0.35 - \$0.70 * 5 = \$10.37$.

Does that make sense? Good! Granted, each company has a different rate of diminishing returns. Some companies need to raise to a power of 0.35, some to a power of 0.50, some to a power of 0.70. This coefficient is easily measured via catalog frequency testing. If you haven't executed tests like this, I have a series of coefficients I use that I can potentially share with you, given my experience with prior catalog analysis projects.

Let's look at what happens for this customer segment, across zero to fifteen catalog mailings:

Catalogs	Cat. Dmd	Org. Dmd	Tot. Dmd	Tot. Profit
0	$0.00	$24.27	$24.27	$8.49
1	$6.87	$24.27	$31.14	$10.20
2	$9.72	$24.27	$33.99	$10.50
3	$11.91	$24.27	$36.18	$10.56
4	$13.75	$24.27	$38.02	$10.51
5	$15.37	$24.27	$39.64	$10.37
6	$16.84	$24.27	$41.11	$10.19
7	$18.19	$24.27	$42.46	$9.96
8	$19.44	$24.27	$43.71	$9.70
9	$20.62	$24.27	$44.89	$9.41
10	$21.74	$24.27	$46.01	$9.10
11	$22.80	$24.27	$47.07	$8.77
12	$23.81	$24.27	$48.08	$8.43
13	$24.78	$24.27	$49.05	$8.07
14	$25.72	$24.27	$49.99	$7.70
15	$26.62	$24.27	$50.89	$7.31

Our actual results showed that this customer received 11.5 catalog mailings in the past year, generating $47.58 demand and $8.62 profit.

The best simulated outcome happens when 3 catalog mailings are sent in a year, generating $36.18 demand and $10.56 profit.

Oh oh.

In other words, this segment of customers is being significantly over-mailed. The first three catalogs generate $36.18 demand and $8.62 profit, while the last 8.5 catalogs generate just $11.40 demand and a loss of $1.96.

This is the magic of "organic demand". Fifteen years of e-commerce success have taught customers to visit our e-commerce websites, unprompted by catalog mailings. We will generate demand without mailing catalogs. Our job is to separate out the organic demand, and then evaluate catalog demand based on a relationship of diminishing returns.

I ran the simulation for one customer. We have more than 176,000 customers in our database. Let's see what the simulation suggests across our twenty-four month housefile!

Decile	HHs	Prediction	Fut. Catlg.	Fut. Orgn.	Fut. Demd.	Mailed	Profit
1	17,671	n/a	$228.66	$152.64	$381.30	20.0	$119.45
2	17,670	n/a	$81.75	$68.26	$150.01	20.0	$38.50
3	17,671	n/a	$36.96	$47.16	$84.12	9.0	$23.14
4	17,670	n/a	$20.04	$31.85	$51.89	5.0	$14.66
5	17,671	n/a	$11.92	$24.27	$36.19	3.0	$10.57
6	17,670	n/a	$8.46	$20.39	$28.85	2.0	$8.70
7	17,671	n/a	$6.91	$17.57	$24.48	2.0	$7.17
8	17,670	n/a	$3.87	$16.31	$20.18	1.0	$6.36
9	17,671	n/a	$3.51	$12.70	$16.21	1.0	$4.97
10	17,670	n/a	$3.22	$13.32	$16.54	1.0	$5.09

Total Catalog Demand	$6,526,527	
Total Organic Demand	$7,147,239	
Total Demand	$13,673,766	
Total Catalogs Mailed	1,130,915	
Total Catalog Cost	$791,641	
Total Profit	$4,216,404	

That is a very different relationship that what was actually being executed!

The simulation wants to mail the top twenty percent of the file twenty catalogs a year, demonstrating a significant increase in profit.

Then, the simulation dramatically reduces the number of catalogs that should be mailed to a customer, with half of the twenty-four month file achieving optimal profitability at just one or two mailings a year.

Let's compare the difference between the deciles in actual catalogs mailed per year, and optimal catalogs mailed per year.

Decile	Actual Catalogs	Optimal Catalogs	Actual Profit	Optimal Profit
1	14.3	20.0	$111.09	$119.45
2	13.7	20.0	$37.99	$38.50
3	13.1	9.0	$22.94	$23.14
4	12.3	5.0	$13.54	$14.66
5	11.5	3.0	$8.62	$10.57
6	10.6	2.0	$6.54	$8.70
7	9.8	2.0	$4.65	$7.17
8	10.0	1.0	$2.99	$6.36
9	7.9	1.0	$2.38	$4.97
10	7.0	1.0	$2.76	$5.09

The existing strategy gradually reduces catalogs as customer quality decreases. The optimal strategy adds catalogs to the top of the file, then dramatically reduces contacts to the bottom 80% of the file.

The result is a business that is just as healthy, from a demand standpoint, but is significantly more profitable with less catalog housefile marketing expense. Take a look!

	Actual	Optimal	Change
Total Catalog Demand	$6,753,938	$6,526,527	-$227,411
Total Organic Demand	$7,147,239	$7,147,239	$0
Total Demand	$13,901,177	$13,673,766	-$227,411
Total Catalogs Mailed	1,946,230	1,130,915	-815,315
Total Catalog Cost	$1,362,361	$791,641	-$570,721
Total Profit	$3,772,695	$4,216,404	$443,709

This is the magic of the "organic percentage". We can measure the amount of demand truly generated by catalog mailings, causing us to make very different mailing decisions. The mailing decisions yield similar demand amounts, a significantly reduced catalog marketing budget, and more profit.

What's not to like about this scenario? What's not to like about a 12% increase in variable operating profit (profit before fixed costs)?

Implementation

The models are not hard to implement. Most of my clients update their customer file on a weekly basis, re-scoring customers into deciles or grades. Most of my clients utilize grades. In our example, grades might look something like this:
- Predicted Catalog Value > $68.00 = Grade of "A"
    - Mail 20 catalogs per year to this grade.
- Predicted Catalog Value between $42.00 and $67.99 = Grade of "B".
    - Mail 7 to 11 catalogs per year to this grade, average = 9.
- Predicted Catalog Value between $11.92 and $41.99 = Grade of "C".
    - Mail 3 to 5 catalogs per year to this grade, average = 4.
- Predicted Catalog Value between $6.91 and $11.91 = Grade of "D".
    - Mail 2 catalogs per year to this grade.
- Predicted Catalog Value between $0.01 and $6.90 = Grade of "F".
    - Mail 1 catalog per year to this grade.

Mailing decisions for "Ds" and "Fs" are straightforward. Either mail these customers the most productive 1-2 catalogs you send to customers, or send customers catalogs that match-up with seasonal buying habits. For instance, if the customer buys swimwear in May, consider mailing the one or two catalogs in or around May, or consider mailing catalogs when there is a significant concentration of swimwear.

Mailing decisions for "As" are straightforward ... mail them everything! The data strongly suggests mailing these customers five more catalogs than are currently available (in our example), so leadership might want to consider adding catalogs or remailing existing catalogs with fresh content on the cover, back cover, and first ten pages.

Mailing decisions for "Bs" and "Cs" are a bit more complex. Odds are that you already know which catalogs are most productive, on the basis of a "comparable segment analysis". In other words, you probably have an RFM segment that you mail every catalog to, and you know the productivity (profit per thousand pages circulated) of that segment in every catalog you mail. Rank-order catalogs from most productive to least productive, choosing the most productive catalogs for customers with a grade of "B" or "C".

Matchbacks

Matchback analytics form the foundation of measurement in the catalog marketing industry. Without matchbacks, we would miss the veritable plethora of online orders that are caused by catalog marketing. Without matchbacks, we would grossly understate the effectiveness of catalog marketing, and we would generate less profit than we generate today.

In the past decade, customer behavior significantly changed. Customers used to need a catalog (or e-mail message or banner ad) to be driven to an e-commerce website. Today, customers enjoy brand loyalty, no longer needing to be advertised to at the levels the customer used to be advertised to. The customer will spend money with us, regardless whether we mail her catalogs or not.

As a result, matchbacks now cause us to over-mail catalogs to most customers. The very problem that matchbacks were designed to solve (online orders not being attributed to catalog marketing) now plagues the matchback, because so many online orders are generated outside of catalog marketing but are incorrectly attributed to catalogs by matchback algorithms.

The methodology outlined in this booklet helps us bypass the problem of matchback analytics. Instead of analyzing each individual catalog, we analyze the overall effectiveness of catalog marketing on an annual basis. This allows us to understand when we are over-mailing or under-mailing different customer segments.

We can't see the over-mailing / under-mailing issue when analyzing catalog results on a drop-by-drop basis. We only observe this issue when analyzing customer behavior on an annual basis.

Criticism

The methodology will be criticized by those in the matchback world, where the concept of organic demand is not well understood. There are many in catalog marketing who believe that a customer is not likely to shop with us if a catalog is not sent to the customer. If you want to prove or disprove this hypothesis, sample 3% of your customer file, and do not mail this segment of customers one single catalog for a six month period of time. You'll quickly learn that customers do order without the need for catalog marketing. In some of the tests I analyze, 75% or more of demand still happens, regardless of catalog mailings. In other tests, 25% of demand still happens, suggesting that catalog marketing is critically important to the success of the business. Either way, you have to execute mail/holdout tests to see where you fall on the continuum.

The methodology will be criticized by math and statistics experts. These folks will not accept my use of a Factor Analysis as a method for assigning customers to Digital Profiles. These folks will not accept my use of random numbers to create the 1/0 indicators used in the Logistics Regression analysis that determines the organic percentage prediction. Let these folks complain, or better yet, encourage these folks to come up with a better solution, and then ask them to sell you their solution for under $10. I've used this methodology in practice. My clients can tell you that the methodology works.

The methodology will be criticized by catalog marketing leaders. I repeatedly run into a large faction of catalog marketing leaders who do not want to accept the new realities of catalog marketing. By and large, catalog marketing is now a niche discipline, appreciated and embraced by a rural customer over the age of 55. Our methodology is perfectly tailored to yielding profit from this audience! If you have demographic data on your customer base, include it in the Digital Profile portion of the analysis, you will see that Digital Profiles with rural customers age 55+ tend to perform well in catalog mailings, and tend to generate minimal amounts of organic demand. Catalog marketing leaders will use this as proof that they don't need to make changes to next year's catalog marketing strategy, they will tell you that catalog marketing is relevant and vibrant. Don't let their argument fool you! When a 29 year old customer buys from your website, the 29 year old isn't asking for a steady diet of 15 catalog mailings a year, the customer was simply looking to have a need met, and you met her need!

The methodology will be criticized by folks as being "geeky", being "too complicated". Well, what's the title of the book? This is a PhD level course in catalog marketing circulation strategy, this isn't a simplistic RFM segmentation scheme that worked exceptionally well in the pre-internet era. You need a methodology like this, and if you are reading this book, you fully understand just how sophisticated customers are today. You know that you need a methodology that dramatically reduces catalog mailings to audiences that are responsive to your brand but not responsive to catalog marketing.

The methodology will be criticized by high-end analytics organizations as being "overly simplistic". These organizations sell expensive solutions, costing $250,000 or $1,000,000 a year. This methodology, which I sold to you for under $10, will get you 90% of the benefit of their solution. They will use a myriad of arguments to convince you that this methodology fails to address relevant issues (how do you deal with a customer who only buys during the Holiday season, or how do you deal with a customer who only buys sale merchandise?). If you want to spend a lot of money to solve those problems, go right ahead, be my guest!

The methodology will be criticized as being nothing more than a "sales pitch" for consulting work that I do. If it were a sales pitch, why would I give away the entire solution for under $10? Now, I'll be perfectly honest. I will send this book to CEOs of leading catalog and retail companies, encouraging them to work with me. But it is more important that these concepts be evangelized in our industry. We're using analysis tools that are twenty years old to attack modern business problems. We need something more sophisticated.

The methodology will be criticized by the folks on Twitter as being "old-school". Well, that's partially right. The methodology uses old science, applied to an old marketing channel. But the methodology is particularly robust. The folks on Twitter would be well-served to integrate online data with offline data. Digital Profiles are perfectly suited for this challenge! Integrate your web analytics data with your customer purchase warehouse, and then incorporate visitation data into your Digital Profiles. You'll find yourself making different marketing decisions among customers who haven't purchased in a long time, but have visited your website in the past fifteen days. Integrate Facebook "Fan" status and Twitter "Follower" status into your customer data warehouse, and you'll suddenly have a rich repository of actionable customer behavior, made actionable via the Digital Profiles you create.

Encouragement

By and large, the marketing industry abandoned catalog marketers five years ago. The "Catalog Conference" became a multi-channel conference without focus or significant attendance, finally dying in 2009. Industry trade journals abandoned catalog marketing, including DMNews, Catalog Age (now Multi-Channel Merchant and a blog that pokes fun at marketers), and Catalog Success.

Even catalog marketers abandoned their passion for catalog marketing. Look at the ACMA (American Catalog Mailers Association), doing so much good for catalogers, and yet, less than 2% of the 15,000+ catalog companies in America bother to muster the $5,000 a year required to support the ACMA. Toss in the obvious environmental concerns, and you have a groundswell of apathy, attacks, and disinterest in catalog marketing.

And yet, catalog marketing works. The e-mail marketing community will laud a 50-to-1 ROI on e-mail marketing, and technically, they are right … you do generate $0.17 of demand for every $0.003 you spend on e-mail marketing, yielding a 50-to-1 return on investment. That being said, I'd take a 4-to-1 return on investment in catalog marketing ($2.00 demand for $0.50 spent) any day of the week!

Catalog marketing works well among the niche audience that appreciates catalog marketing. You just read about a methodology that helps you identify the audience that is most likely to generate profit from catalog marketing. You read about topics that are fairly advanced in the catalog marketing "space". Now take what you've learned, and apply it to your business. Create response models, spending models, and models that measure the organic percentage. Generate unique Digital Profiles for your business. Leverage the Digital Profiles for more than just catalog marketing, use them to analyze online customer behavior! Make strategic changes to your catalog marketing strategy, execute tests, and measure the impact of your changes. Re-invest the money you save in catalog marketing, mailing more catalog customer acquisition names, helping grow your business long into the future. Better yet, re-invest the money in online marketing, social media, and mobile marketing! Re-ignite your passion for a discipline that still generates significant levels of profit among the niche audience that appreciates catalog marketing.

Once you've tried the techniques outlined in this booklet, you will have earned your PhD in Catalog Marketing. That's something to be proud of!!

Consulting

Of course, not everybody can or wants to earn a PhD in catalog marketing strategy.

If you have the resources to attempt implementation of the methodology, I'm confident you'll generate hundreds of thousands of dollars of profit, or even millions of dollars of profit, earning your PhD in Catalog Marketing Strategy.

If you don't have the resources or the desire to earn your PhD, why not earn an honorary PhD in catalog marketing strategy by partnering with me on a consulting project?

I've worked with fifty catalog, retail, and e-commerce businesses in the past four years, a veritable "who's who" of catalog marketing. I've worked with businesses in the UK, in Germany, and in Italy. I've worked with NEMOA members, I've worked with startups, I've worked with 100+ year old brands, I've worked with B2B and B2C brands. I understand the challenges a catalog brand faces in a modern, social media driven marketing environment fueled by mobile devices.

I've worked as an Executive at large companies. I helped shut down a catalog division at Nordstrom and grew total direct-to-consumer sales in spite of the shutdown. I managed circulation strategy at Eddie Bauer, yielding the most profitable year in the direct-to-consumer division. I analyzed the interaction between all catalog titles during my time at Lands' End.

In short, I have the experience to help you earn an Honorary PhD in Catalog Marketing Strategy. Partner with me on a consulting project, and I'll help you achieve your objectives, increasing profit in the process!

Contact Kevin: kevinh@minethatdata.com